Web & Wing

K. Zavorka

Copyright © 2021 K. Zavorka
All rights reserved. No part of this publication may be reproduced, distributed, or transmitted in any form or by any means, including photocopying, recording, or other electronic or mechanical methods, without the prior written permission of the author, except in the case of brief quotations embodied in critical reviews and certain other noncommercial uses permitted by copyright law.
For permission requests, contact the publisher at:

www.Holon.co
ISBN#: 978-1-955342-13-1

Published by:

Holon Publishing & Collective Press
A Storytelling Company
www.Holon.co

This book is dedicated to the under dogs, the mediators, the fighters and the healers. To the ones who know the dark spaces between, the struggle & the beauty of the back story.

To my friends and family for their ongoing love and support, my man and my daughter for forever providing inspiration, and myself for finally seeing this through.

Why am I bound to this earth
like a little dirty thing,
the spider, the fly?
My purpose may be small with web & wing,
but I still dream of sky

It begins
as a flutter in the chest
& beats violently into my stomach;
each surge sends a pitchfork pain
to the tips of my fingers & into my brain —
weeping down my back & whispering down my rib cage.
Such chaos forms from such little wings
who knew,
what could rise from such little things

The fall;
I feel atmospheric.
Like air,
a flutter, a shiver,
until I hit the pavement.
The wind is forced from my lungs
& I lay deflated;
they want me to stay here,
in love,
but I just want to keep falling

I saw the devil at sweet sixteen
in a night that stuck like heat to gasoline
& he drew lines that breathed fire,
like dragons,
I still try
to chase away

Crimson lips, finger tips,
our souls echoing the past.
We lay in fractals on the floor
as our auras dance across the glass,
blushing apparitions smugly mock us from above —
a mirror image of two dazzling spectres
in love

Like fire
we burn through the night,
until dawn fractures the sky.
The ashes whispering past my face remind me:
all that remains are my tired embers
& the smell of smoke
clinging to the air

He held onto me
like rosary, like little beads
to kiss and praise & save him one day,
while I hung from the altar.
But he was a sin wrapped in skin
& I,
just another fucking savior
too tired to listen

He said
to speak no evil,
but the devil rolled off his tongue,
like the sound of the needle to the vinyl,
the soothing song of a velvet lie

I had built him up to Jupiter
& in doing this,
sent him miles away

You smell like cigarettes and September
but I can't shake you with the leaves,
& when autumn turns to winter
where will that leave me?
You'll still be hanging from my boughs,
but with someone else;
& I'm with someone else

You drink me in
holding me heavy in your mouth.
I paint your lips,
wasted red.
Just another pretty thing you've tasted

It's in the days like this
my stomach hurts;
our memories are always obscured, overcast,
where all I want
is to be
loved again

I wrote your name along bay laurels
gifting garlands of hope to the mother deep.
Spirits of the stream cradled it in sodden hands
as the moon regressed in ripples at my feet.
I stood at the meridian of the candlelight and night,
as sirens swore to grant you peace,
& piece by piece they led you
far away from me

He said the heavens lived in me
& he was right,
because planets fell like gods from my eyes
& the tides of titan turned to tear drops
in the night

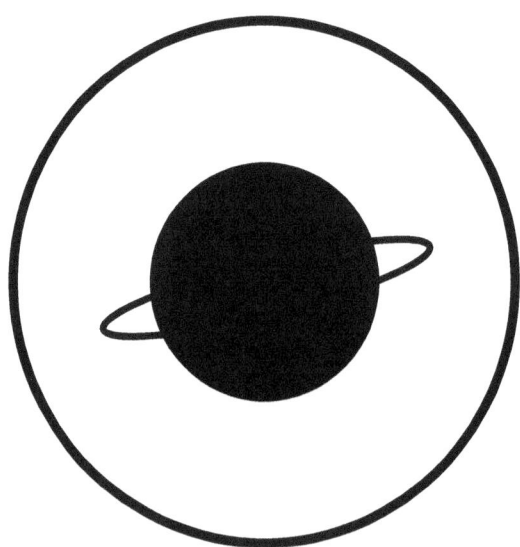

I dreamt
a glass shattered in my mouth
& I swallowed it because I thought it belonged to me.
You asked me if it hurt,
so I lied,
but I woke to the taste of blood
tiptoeing to my ear
& all I hear
are the words I wish I spit out

You traced your footsteps
back to a place
where he once left love
in a bowl by the back door
for your stray, starving little soul,
but love,
he doesn't live there anymore

Some eyes
shine like gold
for fools like you & I;
searching for riches
in reckless hearts

She screams
like a shovel to a shallow grave
but he only speaks in silence,
& lets the stillness
sink her

We were broken hearted like the songs,
love was in the longing,
the cold shoulders, the hot temper;
our dear fathers

In the quiet of morning
you live in a six a.m. song,
I remember the earth now cradles your bones.
The rude awakening
that though this was your home,
once,
we no longer hear your footsteps

Even as your bones are sworn to earth & ash,
the snow's sallow skin
thaws into the veins of the soil;
the leaves begin to shine a tired green.
Citing that even after the darkest winter,
you too, will live again

There was a time
where loneliness sat so heavy in me
that I cast a cord that led me straight to you.
At night I wove you from my body
& spun a web of dreams
of all the things I hoped you'd be and
baptized it in blood & baby's breath
while I cradled you in sunshine & silken thread

She sat smoking in the corner,
a scarlet stigma of who I used to be —
adorned in silver lines singing from her scars.
She watched as I poured my pulse into another;
I picked away the paint chips of her body.
Shades of envy fell to the floor
until an empty wall stood before me,
I chose each colour carefully,
shades of vermillion & emerald green
painting myself in rebellion & gasoline

Tonight is quiet
you stomp in like a war drum.
Each word from your lips
passes from the barrel of a machine gun,
but I have the ammunition
& your forces besieged,
together we lay strewn across the battlefield.
Another pyrrhic victory

I won't be the girl to wear white down the aisle
because I want to wear red on the day that I die;
I won't be that girl that shrugs it off,
my temper is wild and I run with it;
I won't be the girl that your mother loves,
But a decade from now, I'm sure,
I'll still be burning red in the back of your head
while you lay in bed next to "her"

There is a season between
the loving & leaving —
where summer's teeth nip at the heels of November;
where our leaves forget,
but our roots still remember

I have my father's hands,
breaking and mending everything I touch
& if my pact is with the pen
I will wield it as a sword,
because everything in this world
is a fucking war

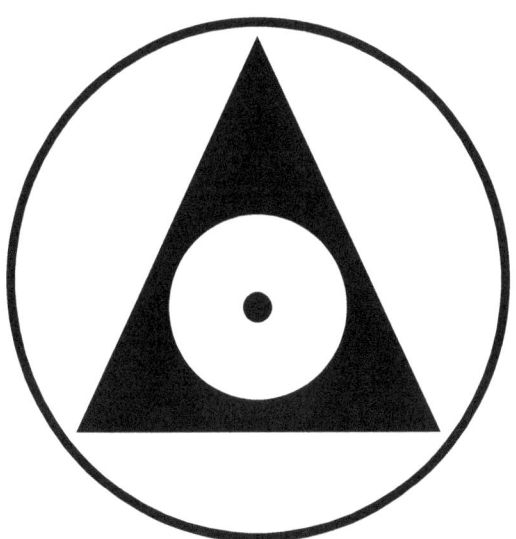

When I was a child
I remember her smile
twice,
Once, when she swam
& once when she ran away from him

I remember,
how it buzzed around in my mouth
like honey,
that little taste of a quiet life
humming in its hive

Our voices smear the silence
shaping the night;
we wait to hear their echo
but there was nothing left to say

It just so happens,
the shades of your lies compliment my eyes.
So paint me as your villain;
I look my best, dressed in deceit

The current swells in my mouth
drowning my words,
I kiss the surface goodbye
as I swallow the undertow

The skin I'm living in finally feels like home,
I keep my demons in my bed so I never sleep alone;
in the silence sits the shadow,
down the barrel burns the shell,
I kiss the devil on his mouth
& send him back to hell

As the snake sheds its skin
we shed our sins
& clothe ourselves
in pretty little lies

I want to be loved like that song,
the one you hear once
& it hurts in all the right places.
So you play me on repeat
over & over
& when you can't hear me,
my pulse will still be ringing in your ears.
I want you to rise and fall with me,
rhythmically,
a major chord, a minor key,
I want to be your fucking symphony

When the day comes
and you try to return to me
know this:
I will not be your home
because I'll always remember
how your eyes lit up
when you tried to burn me to the ground

I was never good at keeping secrets,
so I sent him away like word of mouth

It's not the blood that binds,
but the scar that ties.
So, when I'm down you pull me further
& in all this darkness
we shine brightly

Her eyes flutter
as she falls asleep,
as if she's running
from her dreams

& how quickly they forget
if we don't rise with her,
We die with her

The frost bites its way through
blood & bone,
skin & hair,
forcing our bodies further down
while our breath
still
clings to air

Vanity drips from our lips
to the shallow grave
of a picture frame

We ask ourselves if we are good or bad,
as if we haven't lived
somewhere between heaven & hell
all of our lives

Red wine licks at the seams of her lips,
smoke sips at the mouth of her bottle.
The room was heavy with the smell
of sweat & satin,
velvet & Manhattans.
Her voice a fine French lace,
trembling between the treble & the bass

She had the kind of eyes
that would sit beside you from across the room,
chasing the air out from the mouth
of a hot revolver,
each glare, a flare
flecked within its amber chamber;
I stared into the center & saw a stillness
echoing the sonnet of a smoking gun

She is marigold yellow —
a stroke of canary painted across the sky.
Saffron dances in her hair
like the golden lines in her eye.
Her morning light splits my darkness,
her flaxen blinds my grey.
We ask the dawn to leave us
but beg the sunset stay

She exhales into the surface of the tub,
eyes flickering as ripples are born from her breath,
I tell her one day
she will move the world with a whisper

There is a home in the heart of my mother;
she built it brick by broken brick
& when it grew too heavy,
she turned on the lights and let everyone in,
& I know I lose myself in others,
mending heavy hearts to homes,
but their walls give way to winter,
stone by broken stone

It was cold that day
but they continued to play,
marching through the bitter bite of December.
The city,
reborn in brass & string
mimics a living thing.
Fluorescent lies hung halos in the sky
as the snare spilled its secrets to the street,
while the woodwinds whisper rumours
we would kill to believe

We spun through fields of clovers
chasing fate with dirty feet,
finding faded fortunes & signs in the sky
in crow & cardinal
& crane flying by.
The bright side lived along the edge of four leaves
so we held them in our teeth,
dabbing on dandelion blush,
thinking by chance we could taste
that little thing called luck

I still dream of stepping along the ghats,
the night sweating
from the stone of deities bones
swelling from the walls.
And I felt like something of a demon,
smoking on the shoulder of Shiva
as they dipped their feet in divinity;
washing themselves away with the ones they loved

When I was a child
I would gaze along the cracks of my looking glass
& watch as the sun sank into the brine of the brass,
sending me sailing along the tree line
that stood minding me.
I swung between the chains & dug the silence of that day
into the little scar that rusts along my lifeline

I stopped my reflection & watched
as she licked the salt from her palms;
she reaches for the heavens
as I chase her back to hell

We still don't know how to stand
within these four walls,
when we've grown taller
than the tales they told
& this place they call
home

There's a little war in her,
I see it
in the red of her eyes when mars rises
to the surface of her iris
& burns beneath the waves

Like air
she would come and go,
as zephyrs blow beneath the bane
of nightshade and narcissus,
the down of dandelions wade upon her lips
as she whispers
what love is to the western wind

We painted our pain into paper cranes
& hung them from the ceiling,
mosaics manifest as falling feathers
as lights liberate slender wings along the walls.
They wisp away by snow & starlight
their shadows winking from the window panes,
reminiscing the spirits of December

I saw my sister today;
her smile split her face like cracked amber,
the scars hiding in her hairline shimmered
 gold.
She knew my eyes since I was a child
& asked me if I had been crying;
I squeezed more blood from stone.
So she read me the story we both knew
tethered in leather & lead,
I saw her bound to that bed again,
skin & bone,
when she asked me if she could come home…

The line between us is inherent.
My mother's blood lives in your veins;
they still call you sister,
but no sister remains

We carved secrets on their skin
& watched the sun seep in
sketching spirals of solar streams & sunbeams,
each line a lifetime
etched in oak and pine,
we trace the rings along our lips
& kiss the years goodbye

We stood staring at the sun,
you said pretty girls deserve pretty things.
So we searched through swollen beams
& when I closed my eyes
orbs of red & green
hung against my eyelids.
You asked, what did I see
& it was your hollow outline
blindly loving me

His heart hums
a tune that's stuck at the tip of my tongue
but mine's a drum
that only sings the sound of leaving

Psyche
lights my way,
& by curve of bow & quiver
my heart sways.
Eternal is the severed line
that lies between your heart & mine,
& from the tip of cupid's arrow
we drink nectar and ambrosia

The fever from the flame
as darkness follows light,
our secrets on our skin
from the gliding velvet knife,
the sting that follows sweet
as the thistles milk turns sour,
a kiss, where tongue & tooth meet
the thorn & silken flower

We built cathedrals out of cupid's bows & curls
as if innocence held the riches of the world.
Searching for revelation on the surface of our skin,
but I dug deeper in.
To the serpent in the center of my stomach
blossoming from the blood of eve,
I tore down his temple
& watched
as god gushed out of me

Its leaves taste the fool on my fingers
as I pick away at its petals,
sowing lies dressed in white,
the oxen eye tells me he loves me

I searched for myself in white lines,
& the light at the end of every deal,
lost in the lies of synthetic eyes
that rose from the bottom of a bottle
& sank against the bathroom floor.
The walls dilated, deflated,
sick on a summer night
& smothered in the sound of sirens;
he said
"little girl, you're too pretty to die."

I can smell love coming,
like spirits
buzzing,
on the breath of a man
who's licked the wick of a fire bottle —
burning napalm in the night

She rose like belladonna
from the night,
shades
of violent violet
sipping on the shadow of the sun
like a flower in February

That woman
held her pain in her palm
like the dust of bloodborne diamonds,
in prisms,
too precious to part with

I remember high-rises
but not the kind
made from steel & stone,
but the ones we traced in sweat,
flesh & bone,
between breaths,
strung out & scraping the sky

She tamed many monsters,
most of them men
that sat like ghosts in her throat
concealed within conscience,
but Venus rose for her
with cupids bows
& married the Moon to Mercury,
promising the sky & sea
that the line between them
would be their horizon

Words have always been my weapon,
So I spit them as venom
or swallow my own poison

I too,
began to sing
with the birds of spring
far before winter's storms came shrieking back
& the howls of heartbreak rushed my lips,
silencing the ides

You settled into me
like a lost love,
holding your place with the heavy things
in a heart beating on highs
& fell to the bottom
skipping against the sides,
sinking like a stone

I've always been a high roller
blindly betting on the joker when I see him;
something about snake eyes & smokin aces
& the little lies behind his smile
that spin the cylinder of my roulette heart

To be a careful creature
was never in my cards,
I learnt that when I was small.
When I fell off the wall & into the wild,
the second something pretty stained my vision,
they knew it then,
that I had an eye for fickle things,
& in every fortune
I'd always draw the fool

I always locked my heart in the shadows,
caged away in lead & graphite grey
she climbed the walls like a flower in the shade,
& the song she sang
the day I let her beat from my chest,
when she was always told
she was too wild to wander

We dance
in our living rooms
to different tunes of tragedy,
& even in the saddest songs
& loneliest lullabies,
we still listen for love

And as I sat pretty
waiting for a sorry to slip through his teeth,
I thought how it must feel —
for a man like him
to ask a woman like me
for forgiveness

Smiling through my teeth
wasn't for me.
So I learned to bare them
each time I was told to bite my tongue,
as if I would ever tell the serpent in my mouth to tremble
in the midst of a man
when I could scare him instead

You & I just want to make sparks fly,
well I'm gunpowder & you're always loaded.

& after him
I set my sights so high
into a cemetery of stars;
burning lines along tie dye skies
across heaven's ink blue body,
where I searched for angels
& found a devil with a halo

She scales the walls of her bones,
slinking out from under the sheets;
I find her stained in stardust,
love drunk on moonshine,
& wearing the rings of Saturn
she marries the night

& she danced
like a rumor through the night,
an omen
dressed in light,
star-crossed
& starry-eyed

He finds me along the tail of darkness,
in the lithe light that drivels down
& lusts after my shadow —
my shadow who feigns
in the sweat that breaks
between fever dreams & night's teeth,
wake's morning
to starve the smell of my footsteps,
& in the dark, he waits
to dream again,
to cry wolf

I want a man like the sky,
who speaks to me in sandstone & magnolia,
fucks like thunder sounds & rain tastes.
Loves in shades
royal, slate
when I'm baby blue
sometimes grey

My skin has more memories
of storms than dreams,
of days where hurricanes
still
chant after me,
& the tears undress & break me open,
like earth after rain,
like love after pain

He says I'm sweet shame,
cherry stained;
calls me lovely, when I listen,
calls me late,
like expired midnight;
names me devil at dawn,
says he wants me, reckless
but lord knows
the lies we live for love

She wasn't a woman
who would purr in your ear like acoustics,
or sway along the paint like a muse of Degas,
but a woman whose name
settles in your skin like black ink,
to remind you
that some things stay,
even after they walk away from you

Little flower,
your beauty will not seduce light's temper
nor charm the egos of the day.
You do not sway the wind to sing
& the moon will not savor your sleepy gaze
over those who lust after it.
But your earth will always hold you
as a secret, spoken once then sworn sacred;
your earth
will always hold you

He serenades me in swollen breath,
pains for me, his pretty poison
his lazy gaze, that dilates
then pulls back like highs and lows
& between my thighs,
we day-dream

How sweet it tastes,
when a wish escapes our lips
with such artless abandon,
then returns to us
a kiss of luck,
by chance

The last lesson
I learned from a man,
was the second I gave him
a way out & his eyes ran,
only to crawl back to me
as a thing he called
"better"

My heart starves
for a pulse to warm the static space
in the quiet nights between
streetlights that still glamour my gazing shadow
& the heat that feeds me to the flames

She moved like rainwater,
like torrents that burn the backsplash of the day,
in azure swells & fevered rays
that fall & break against sun's set,
in watercolour,
stained in summer sweat

I search for peace
in the quietest places I can dream up,
but even in dead sleep
the dead speak

The day I jumped in too deep
I heard them say
"Sink or swim,"
& that sank deeper
than the water in the windpipe

Hope is a ghost,
a dream with a name,
I dare not speak aloud

Hope laughed along the walls one day,
like a song singing
down these empty halls,
like liquid love.
I spilled it out, I licked it up;
I spoke its name & it sank away
like water stains on ceilings,
seeping into the restless plaster
of my idle heart

& the stars aligned
like gunfire in the sky,
like life spilling onto pavement
into crimson cracked streets
that their feet still scream upon.
To trade your blind eye for an eye to see,
the difference between
choke holds, bullet holes,
& peace

How the light lit those eyes up
like smoke screens and nicotine,
& provoked a summer day
that burned like a memory I inhaled,
familiar

I searched for safety
in loose lips
& tested his tongue for a word,
too heavy
for his empty mouth to carry

I've learned to erase
the ways I tricked my body to love him,
the way my eyes only searched for empty, for lacking,
so I could fill his cold vacant center with febrile warmth,
just to be spilled from his stingy dimples,
just to be the girl he smiled for

Shaky words whisper into 5:00 am
& hang over my head,
like cotton candy skies still sticky from the night before.
Still stoned on the taste of together,
though sober slithers in like a stranger;
I still can't feel the bottom
even when I'm coming down.

I will never know alone
like I did the night before I met him,
when I bloomed under the moon in May
& buried kings beneath my pillow

I left today dreaming,
I fed it scent of evergreen
& filled its belly with laughter
so it no longer hungered for love.
I bathed it in honey,
pity & promises,
& swaddled it in silk of the finest sympathies.
I carried its tired soul to sleep with me,
telling it of who we would be tomorrow,
as its balmy breath clung to the still of day & the night
came to carry its eyes away with it

I've chewed through truths
with razorblade sides
& I've stomached lies
that have burned my belly like bile,
So the shit you feed me
won't be the worst I've ever tasted

Remember,
It comes in pieces
like broken brick
& burning bridges,
like the wars that climbed
like fire then fell
& peace was built
on a hope in hell

It was that kind of love,
the kind you carry with you like a headstone,
& even though it's been dead for so long,
you still can't break the ground to bury it.

For a godless woman like me
this sure feels a lot like praying,
as I lay in bed begging
for our chance to kiss & tell.

It's easy to be the tough one,
flaunting pain like a trophy,
licking triumph
off the edge of the blade,
until the blood bragging from our tongues
bleeds into words,
reminding us to speak softer to the knife,
& when it starts to hurt,
say mercy

I want to see my name
moan along his mouth
when he thinks of flames
& wicked things,
I want to see him burn his tongue
on a woman written in firewater

About the Author

Kat Zavorka is the author of "Web & Wing." A collection of poetry which echoes in the hearts of its readers – evoking reflection on love, loss, redemption and the beauty of climbing back up from the bottom.

www.ingramcontent.com/pod-product-compliance
Lightning Source LLC
Chambersburg PA
CBHW040834190426
43197CB00046B/2970